UNDERSTANDING AND PRAYING FOR

Revival

PERSONAL JOURNAL

SELWYN HUGHES AND IAN SEWTER

CWR

Published 2006 by CWR, Waverley Abbey House, Waverley Lane, Farnham, Surrey GU9 8EP, England.

Concept development, editing, design and production by CWR

Printed in England by Linneys

ISBN-13: 978-1-85345-394-6

ISBN-10: 1-85345-394-3

CONTENTS

CONTENTS

HOW TO USE

To use this guide most effectively, set aside perhaps one and a half hours for each session. The DVD clip should be watched at the start of a session, and will normally take around fifteen to twenty minutes. In this booklet which accompanies the DVD, there are a number of discussion starters. This section could take another twenty to thirty minutes. This would then lead into a time of prayer – for which a number of suggestions have been given.

Finally, there are some useful notes and Bible references for each person to read between sessions, finishing with a personal journal page. This helps to reinforce and apply the message of each section. Try and read the notes and answer the first two questions on the journal page as soon as possible after the session. Do refer back to both the notes and suggestions for prayer during the week, and prior to meeting again, complete the last question.

The first session covers the characteristics of revival and the other three sessions highlight the major obstacles to revival. The aim of this resource is not simply that we learn more about revival and prayer but that we actually become people who pray for revival.

INTRODUCTION

In 1965 CWR was founded by Selwyn Hughes with the primary objective of encouraging people to pray for both personal and corporate revival, and deepen their understanding of the Word of God. Much of our work over the last years has been to prepare God's people for revival.

Selwyn always felt that God's call on his life was to elevate the spiritual vision of the Church to focus its gaze on revival – on God pouring out His Holy Spirit on a nation, so that thousands of Christians are revived and thousands might come to know Jesus Christ as their personal Saviour. Our task is to provide the prayer ramp over which His purposes can pass – hence this special resource to encourage prayer for revival. It is based upon the Why Revival Waits message which Selwyn gave in cities around the British Isles over a four-year period. Over 9,000 people heard this stirring and challenging message – culminating at the Worthing Tabernacle where filming of the DVD took place in 2004, capturing this vital word for today's Church.

How, then, do revivals begin? One school of thought says, 'Revival is a sovereign act of God and there is absolutely nothing we can do to make it happen.' Others say, 'Revival can happen any time the Church wants it – provided she is willing to pay the price.' Revival is a sovereign act of God in the sense that He alone can produce it, but He deigns to hand over to His people the responsibility of bringing it down from heaven to earth on the wings of fervent, believing prayer. Our own prayer at CWR is that as you use this resource you too will be inspired to pray for the revival that God wants to pour out on His people.

SESSION 01

Understanding revival

HAVING WATCHED THE VIDEO, NOW CONSIDER TOGETHER:

What are the characteristics of revival?

How do you feel the modern Church compares to the Early Church?

Do any of the characteristics of revival concern you?

Why might the message of the cross not be as effective today?

How can we interest a modern generation in Scriptures that were written over 2,000 years ago?

01 Suggestions for prayer

Pray that God would give you a greater understanding of revival and how He wants to use you.

Have we been asleep? Ask God to wake us from our slumber and to the need for revival.

Pray for a fresh vision of God – a vibrant, palpable sense of His presence.

Pray that God would not allow us to settle – settling for less than He has for us.

Pray that God would open our eyes to sin, and for people's hearts to receive His message of love and salvation.

Pray that the Holy Spirit would fill you and God's Church with power, boldness and infectious enthusiasm.

Ask God to raise up others with an interest in revival who will pray for God to pour out His Holy Spirit again, and for a fresh vision for revival in your life, church and the locality in which you live.

01 Understanding revival

READINGS: JOEL 2:28–29; ACTS 2:1–14, 36–47

We must acknowledge that there are different views on the subject and definition of revival. However, all Christians would be able to agree that God has something bigger in His heart for us than we are at present experiencing. Read through the 'Brief History of Revivals' on the inside back cover of this booklet to be inspired by the past and encouraged that God can do again in our day what He has done in generations past.

So, what is revival? What does it look like? We may say from a study of the Scriptures and Church history, that true revival has a number of characteristics. Firstly, there is an *extraordinary sense of God's presence and of His holiness*. Now, we can sometimes sense the presence of God in church perhaps over a considerable period of time. In revival, however, people have been gripped by an awareness of God in their own homes and places of work, and have fallen down confessing even long-forgotten or previously tolerated sins exposed by the Holy Spirit.

There is often *extraordinary preaching and an extraordinary understanding of the cross*. The cross of Christ always takes on a new and precious meaning in times of revival. People see the cross, not in general terms: 'He died for us' (Rom. 5:8), but in personal terms: 'He died for me' (Gal. 2:20). The cross becomes so real that the wounds, bruises and insults Jesus suffered provoke such deep personal sorrow that there is a deeper consecration and devoted love to such a Saviour. This is not just evangelism where the evangelist is appealing for souls but an *extraordinary move of God* where people are 'cut to the heart' and cry out, 'What can we do to be saved?' (Acts 2:37; 16:30).

Often in revival there are *extraordinary physical occurrences*. At Pentecost there was a mighty wind, fire and speaking in unknown languages. In other revivals, such as in 1859 in Ulster, there were 'strikings down', when people would fall to the ground and lie motionless for hours under the power of God's presence. It is not always clear why God would do this, nonetheless we need to make sure that we do not undermine the Spirit by our intellectualism and unwillingness to accept the supernatural events that generally accompany revival.

One of the effects of revival is an *extraordinary interest in prayer and in reading the Scriptures*. After Pentecost the apostles decided to abstain from their administrative duties so they could give themselves continually to prayer and the ministry of the Word (Acts 6:4). In today's Church, many Christians are content to let their pastors or elders do the praying and studying for them, but in revival each Christian finds his or her heart leaping towards prayer and reading God's Word.

Another characteristic is *extraordinary fervour and excitement*. The dull, apathetic attitude which is present in some churches today, was a thing unknown in the first-century Christian community. They were gripped by intense excitement and a spirit of expectation. The same power that had raised Christ from the grave and elevated Him to the heavens at the right hand of the Father was working in them with all its quickening might. In revival, Christians sometimes have to defend themselves from a charge of being drunk. Today we are more dignified, sophisticated, respectable and sober – and even more in need of revival.

Let us understand that our prayers and expectations for revival can be based upon the greatest manifestation of the Holy Spirit the world has ever known – Pentecost. Don't be concerned by theologians who claim that Pentecost was simply a one-off experience, never to be repeated. Of course there is only one Pentecost, but it is also a model of what revival may look like in our own generation. The revivals that have taken place over the last two to three hundred years all contain one or more of the elements that were present at Pentecost. In some, the dominant feature has been conviction of sin, in others, abounding joy, and in others, amazing supernatural events. Let us be prepared for any or all of these. After all, God can do as He chooses. 'Don't suppress the Spirit, and don't stifle those who have a word from the Master. On the other hand, don't be gullible. Check out everything, and keep only what's good' (1 Thess. 5:19–21, *The Message*).

01

My personal journey of revival

The key truths I have learnt or been reminded of are:

As a result I intend to:

As I look back on this week I would like to note:

02 SESSION

Managing without God

HAVING WATCHED THE VIDEO, NOW CONSIDER TOGETHER:

Why is pride such a significant obstacle to revival?

What is the difference between self-effacement and true humility?

How can we humble ourselves?

How do you ensure that your strengths do not become objects of pride?

How did God respond to the attitudes of the Pharisee and the tax collector (see Luke 18:9–14)?

Why could parts of the modern Church be compared to the church of Laodicea (see Rev. 3:14–17)?

02 Suggestions for prayer

Give thanks: spend some time acknowledging to God His greatness and the greatness of His creation.

Acknowledge to God our inability to save ourselves and that we are lost without Christ.

Give God the glory for good things that have happened to you and your church.

Confess any areas of pride and independence in your own heart.

Confess any attitudes of pride and independence in the Church.

continued ...

Ask God to help you know His Word better. Take steps to determine to read it this week.*

Ask God to reveal His plans to us, rather than merely asking Him to bless our clever ideas.

If pride is the greatest impediment to revival and revival is our greatest need – what should we do? Spend time now before God asking Him to reveal the next steps for you this week.

* If you do not currently use any Bible reading notes, visit www.cwr.org.uk to discover publications that may help you.

02 Managing without God

READING: LUKE 18:9–14

In 2 Chronicles 7:14, God puts humility before prayer with good reason. Pride is one of the biggest barriers to God having His way in His Church. Unless we first humble ourselves, any prayer is simply us coming before God on our terms and asking Him to bless our ideas, rather than acknowledging our total dependency on Him, for without Him we can do nothing (John 15:5).

The old theologians put pride at the head of the list of deadly sins. 'Pride,' said one preacher, 'is the primal sin. Little as we know of the life of the angels, there is evidence for believing that pride led to the revolt of Satan in heaven' (Isa. 14:11–15; Ezek. 28:1–19). Pride in our own abilities, self-interest and a desire for independence is certainly at the forefront of many a revolt against God. You see, if you have pride you can rely too much on your own abilities and ideas and be too proud to acknowledge that you need another's help. Therefore, you become reluctant to ask for it or you merely ask for 'a little bit of help'.

However, 'God opposes the proud but gives grace to the humble' (James 4:6). Contrast this with the fabulously wealthy and successful King David who acknowledged that, 'Wealth and honour come from you ... Everything comes from you, and we have given you only what comes from your hand' (see 1 Chron. 29:10–16).
One who learned this lesson the hard way was

Nebuchadnezzar. Twelve months after he failed to respond to God's warning of his pride, he said, '"Is not this the great Babylon I have built as the royal residence, by my mighty power and for the glory of my majesty?" ... Immediately ... He was driven away from people and ate grass like cattle. His body was drenched with the dew of heaven until his hair grew like the feathers of an eagle and his nails like the claws of a bird.' Only when he humbly repented and acknowledged God's sovereignty were his sanity and kingdom restored (Dan. 4).

The Pharisee in Luke 18 approached God concerned only about himself and his position. In fact, Jesus revealed that the Pharisees did not pray to receive from God but to demonstrate their supposed religious superiority and be admired by people (Matt. 6:1–5; 23:1–12). Self-centredness is a blight that affects both the redeemed and the unredeemed. Because we are Christians it does not automatically mean that we are protected from the disease of self-interest. How many times have you allowed yourself rather than God to have the last word about an issue or spiritual challenge in your life? When pride is present, then everything that arises has an immediate self-reference. There can be no real victory in Christians' lives until they have found victory over pride. The phrase 'humble yourself' suggests that an act of the will is necessary. God can humble us, but how much more meaningful it becomes when we do it ourselves. Are you a proud person? Then do something today to trample on your pride. Pride has many destructive characteristics, but its most devestating is the fact that it blocks the way to revival.

It has been suggested that humility is one of the most misunderstood of all Bible concepts. The world confuses humility with self-belittlement, lack of ambition, an inferiority complex or a 'servile, grovelling spirit'. True humility is found not when you stoop to be low, but when you stand at your full height against some higher ability that reveals the smallness of your own supposed greatness. Phillip Brooks said, 'Stand at your highest, then look to Christ and go away forever humble.'

Moses was said to be, 'more humble than anyone else on the face of the earth' (Num. 12:3). Yet he opposed the greatest leader on earth, led a nation of over a million and ordered judicial executions. Moses' humility was defined by his relationship as an obedient servant of the most high God. In other words, he was prepared to humbly obey whatever God told him to do and he acknowledged that without God he could do nothing. One of the key indicators of a truly humble person is the way he or she respects the word of God by humbly receiving and obeying it (James 1:21; 3:13). This is why the humble person trembles at His word (Isa. 66:2), not out of a sense of fear but one of respect and desire to fully obey it from an attitude of reverence and a desire to please God.

02

My personal journey of revival

The key truths I have learnt or been reminded of are:

As a result I intend to:

As I look back on this week I would like to note:

SESSION 03

Call me when the fire falls

HAVING WATCHED THE VIDEO, NOW CONSIDER TOGETHER:

How does our view of God affect our prayer life and what changes do you need to make in order to become a more prayerful person?

Why is persistence in prayer important? (See Exod. 17:8–13; Luke 18:1–8.)

Share a testimony of answered prayer.

Why can we pray to God with confidence? (See John 14:13–14; Heb. 4:14–16; 1 John 3:21–24.)

Why is prayer sometimes difficult and what has helped your own prayer life that could also encourage others?

Why do we not receive from God? (See James 4:1–3.)

03 Suggestions for prayer

One of the key aspects of prayer is thankfulness, so spend some time praising God for who He is and what He has done in your life.

Pray like Moses to 'see the face of God' – that is to simply enjoy His presence without requiring anything from Him.

Ask God to impress the importance of prayer on His people and His Church.

Think how you would feel if there were a local disaster, and in that sense of concern and desperation pray that your friends and neighbours will be saved and your church be a beacon of hope.

Ask God to help you deepen your prayer life by helping you to understand and practise different types of prayer.

What local or national issues concern you that you would like God to change?

Aim this week to extend your experience of prayer in some way. For some this may be by praying out loud in a group, spending thirty minutes in prayer, writing a prayer, fasting a meal, etc.

03 Call me when the fire falls

READINGS: LUKE 11:1–13; 1 TIMOTHY 2:1; JAMES 4:1–3

John Wesley once famously said, 'God does nothing in this world redemptively except through prayer.' C.S. Lewis compared history to a play where the scenery and general outline are fixed by the playwright, but certain things are left for the actors and actresses to improvise. This illustration has some weaknesses, but in general it represents a fair picture of how God has set up the universe. God has foreordained certain things to happen, of course, but above and beyond that there are things which will only come to pass if we pray. Revival is one of these things. What an exciting prospect this holds out for us; co-operating with God in believing prayer, we can team up with Him and watch in breathless admiration and amazement as He responds to our prayers to change the world.

However, many Christians feel discouraged – even guilty – about their prayer lives. They become disheartened because they have tried to copy the style, timing and pattern of other people's prayers only to find that they did not suit their personality or circumstances. We need to develop our own pattern of prayer, one that is appropriate to us, for nobody can pray your prayers better than you.

Another obstacle is a faulty view of God. How do *you* honestly see God? Over the years that question has been put to many believers and the answers have been surprising. 'I see God as distant, uncommunicative and judgmental,' said one. You don't need three guesses to know what kind of prayer life that person experienced. Look again at Luke 11; it tells us that, contrary to what many of us may think, God is a loving Father who delights to answer prayer. The Almighty is not mean or stingy and enjoys giving us everything we need. Is there any parent who does not delight to give their child something they know is good for them? Now multiply that feeling a million times and you get a faint picture of how God feels when we ask Him for the power to live the life He has called us to live. We do not have to overcome God's reluctance; we simply have to lay hold on His highest willingness.

We must also face the fact, however, that we do not always give prayer its right priority in our lives. Matthew 6:25–34 encourages us to seek God's kingdom first rather than being preoccupied with things like fashion and food. *The Message* version of Matthew 26:41, when Jesus rebuked the disciples for sleeping instead of praying, says: 'Stay alert; be in prayer so you don't wander into temptation without even knowing you're in danger. There is a part of you that is eager, ready for anything in God. But there's another part that's as lazy as an old dog sleeping by the fire.' Maybe we need to overcome our spiritual lethargy and, like Jesus, rise early in the morning or set aside other special times to pray (Mark 1:35; Luke 5:16).

Someone has said that in the Gospels we read much about prayer, but it is mostly the prayer life and teachings of Jesus. In the Acts of the Apostles however, following Pentecost, we find the disciples in one prayer meeting after another. What does this say to us? Surely this: that the coming of the Spirit set fire to the prayer lives of the early believers. It ought to be the same with us. If we claim to be filled with the Spirit, then one evidence ought to be the place we give to fervent, believing intercessory prayer.

There are several types of prayer. For example, thanksgiving is when we appreciate God for what He has done. Praise worships God for who He is – a loving, caring, holy Creator. Petition and supplication refer primarily to the requests we ask of Him in respect of our own needs and those closest to us. We can also 'seek the Lord' and 'wait upon the Lord' when we spend time in His presence with no other desire than simply to be with Him and hear what He has to say to us. Intercession is different. It stands between a holy God and a sinful people and pleads that God will pour out His mercy and blessing on others rather than the judgment we all so clearly deserve. Revival praying is intercessory prayer, and a lost art amongst many of God's people. May we, like the early disciples, be taught to pray.

03

My personal journey of revival

The key truths I have learnt or been reminded of are:

As a result I intend to:

As I look back on this week I would like to note:

SESSION 04

Why revival waits

HAVING WATCHED THE VIDEO, NOW CONSIDER TOGETHER:

Why do we need God to search our hearts?

Why are our 'wicked ways' an obstacle to revival?

Why might a casual attitude to the Word of God lead to adopting modern thinking?

What are the 'wicked ways' that Christians might follow, or that might be seen within the Christian community?

Why is it important to fix our eyes on God rather than on His Church and church activities?

You can be a vanguard for revival – remember 'Revival is heaven sent – but it's a fire lit on earth' – what now are you going to do?

04 Suggestions for prayer

Ask God to make His Church pure and a holy shining example of a city on a hill to those around who live in darkness.

Ask God to search your own heart and the heart of the Church to reveal and keep us from walking in 'wicked ways'.

Thank God for His Word and pray that it, rather than public opinion, will be the major influence in your life. Determine to read it every day.

Confess any wrong attitudes towards Christians of other denominations and pray for God to bless them.

continued ...

Bring before God areas where you feel that you may have wrongly accepted the world's standards.

As appropriate, confess 'wicked ways' that you have personally followed.
(This could be in private or with a trusted prayer partner.)

Ask God to pour out His Holy Spirit on the Church and the country so that a new tide of revival would flood across our nation – that He might heal our land.

04 Why revival waits

READINGS: ISAIAH 1:15–17; 5:20; MALACHI 3:6–10; JAMES 2:1–10

Can it be true that God's people have wicked ways? Perhaps the Lord meant careless ways or formal ways – surely not *wicked ways*? The Bible says 'wicked ways' (2 Chron. 7:14). Perhaps we Christians have so learned to rationalise our actions and behaviour that we do not realise quite how wicked they really are.

The tendency in this day and age is to let ourselves off lightly whenever we have done wrong. We tend to use such euphemisms as, 'Well, the only one I hurt was myself', or 'It is not that important or wrong'. But *any* violation of a biblical principle is immensely serious. When we pass on a juicy bit of gossip concerning someone who has erred and strayed – that is a *wicked* way. When we criticise and condemn those who have spiritual oversight for us, rather than bring them before God in prayer – that is a *wicked* way. When we wound others by our words or actions, and fail to ask their forgiveness – that is a *wicked* way. When the acquisition of money dominates our thinking and crowds out eternal things – that is a *wicked* way. When we watch degrading films or read morally debilitating literature – that is a *wicked* way. When we show favouritism – that is a *wicked* way.

Worldliness is another *wicked* way. Some think of worldliness in terms of going to pubs, clubs, cinemas or football matches and so on, but really it is an attitude of mind – it means thinking like the world. Instead of letting Scripture be our standard and guide, we tend to form conclusions based on the latest newspaper article, public opinion survey or television programme. Where is fulfilment to be found? Apparently in a house makeover, foreign holiday, new car, latest fashion, computer accessory or even a bar of chocolate. Now none of these things are wicked ways in themselves but we must remember to be careful that they do not become idols (Col. 3:5; 1 John 5:21).

Even in Paul's day he had to warn believers against 'many foolish and harmful desires that plunge men into ruin and destruction. For the love of money is a root of all kinds of evil.' In fact 'Some people, eager for money ... wandered from the faith' (1 Tim. 6:9–10). What is acceptable in our world? Apparently, same-sex marriages, godless philosophies and the deification of sports stars and celebrities.

Take another view held by the world and also by many Christians – the standard for all behaviour is love. No, says the Bible, the standard for behaviour is truth (Rom. 2:2). Slowly but surely I believe Christians in this generation are allowing the world's opinions to mould their thinking and are becoming more and more of the world.

Can these things, and there are many others, go on in the hearts of those who claim to be Christians – the hearts of God's own people called by His name? Unfortunately they can. If we are guilty of any of these wicked ways then let us, here and now, repent of them and have done with them.

As the people of God, the world has a right to expect us to be different.

Following our final session, let me draw a conclusion which is this: nothing else but an extraordinary move of God can meet the urgent need of the Church at this time. Evangelism, conferences, seminars and other church activities, while important and necessary, are inadequate in themselves to arrest the attention of an unbelieving world. *God must come down and visit us again with mighty Holy Spirit power.*

Bishop Wilberforce wrote these encouraging words,

> We look at some mighty estuary which the retiring tide has left bare of water. We see little trickling rivulets wearing their scarcely appreciable way through the resisting banks of that yielding ooze. The man who knows not the secrets of the tide and the influence by which God governs nature would say, 'how can you expect to see that great expanse covered?' But high in the heavens, the unseen Ruler shall bring in the tides of the surrounding ocean.

General Booth gave similar advice to his eldest daughter when she was discouraged on a foreign mission field: 'Take your eyes off the waves and fix them on the tide.' Christian friend, take heart. The unseen Ruler has willed the revival of His people. But He looks to us to 'prepare the way of the Lord' through the influence of prayer so that 'the earth will be full of the knowledge of the LORD as the waters cover the sea' (Isa. 11:9).

04

My personal journey of revival

The key truths I have learnt or been reminded of are:

As a result I intend to:

As I look back on this week and this series I would like to note: